I0815356

History of the Titanic

Making Titanic the Movie

by Julie Murray

Level 1 – Beginning
Short and simple sentences with familiar words or patterns for children who are beginning to understand how letters and sounds go together.

Level 2 – Emerging
Longer words and sentences with more complex language patterns for readers who are practicing common words and letter sounds.

Level 3 – Transitional
More developed language and vocabulary for readers who are becoming more independent.

abdobooks.com

Published by Abdo Zoom, a division of ABDO, PO Box 398166, Minneapolis, Minnesota 55439.

Printed in the United States of America, North Mankato, Minnesota.
102024
012025

Photo Credits: Alamy, Everett Collection, Getty Images, Shutterstock
Production Contributors: Kenny Abdo, Jennie Forsberg, Grace Hansen, John Hansen
Design Contributors: Candice Keimig, Neil Klinepier

Library of Congress Control Number: 2024936562

Publisher's Cataloging in Publication Data

Names: Murray, Julie, author.
Title: Making Titanic the movie / by Julie Murray
Description: Minneapolis, Minnesota : Abdo Zoom, 2025 | Series: History of the Titanic | Includes online resources and index.
Identifiers: ISBN 9781098287252 (lib. bdg.) | ISBN 9781098287955 (ebook) | ISBN 9781098288303 (Read-to-me ebook)
Subjects: LCSH: Motion pictures--Juvenile literature. | Shipwrecks--North Atlantic Ocean--Juvenile literature. | Drama films--Juvenile literature. | Historic ships--Juvenile literature. | Titanic (Steamship)--Juvenile literature.
Classification: DDC 910.9163--dc23

Table of Contents

Making *Titanic* the Movie

Titanic is one of the most successful movies of all time. Filming began in July 1996.

James Cameron was the film's **director**. He took many trips to the **RMS** *Titanic* wreckage. These trips **inspired** him.

The movie tells the story of two people, Rose and Jack, who meet on the ship and fall in love. They come from very different backgrounds.

Jack Dawson is played by Leonardo DiCaprio. He is a charming, poor artist. He won his tickets to board the ship in a card game.

Rose DeWitt Bukater is played by Kate Winslet. She is a **socialite** who is engaged to a man she does not love.

Cameron paid close attention to detail while filming. He made sure all the décor and **props** were true to the time.

A life-size **replica** of the **RMS** *Titanic* was built for the film. It could be tilted and rotated to bring the sinking scene to life.

Filming ended in March of 1997. The movie took eight months and cost $200 million to make.

Box Office Hit!

Titanic opened on December 19, 1997. It was an immediate success! It won 11 Academy Awards.

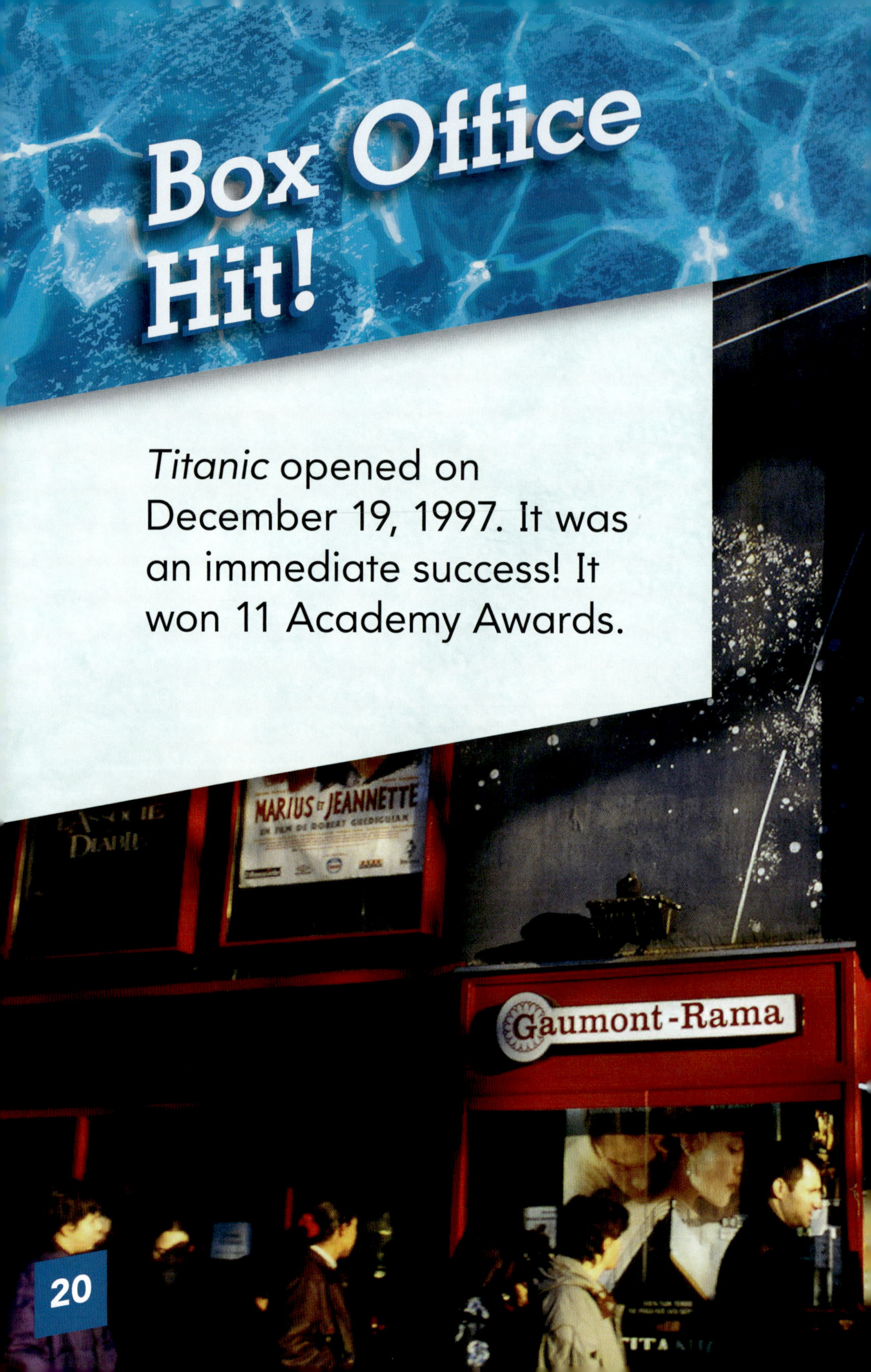

RIEN SUR TERRE NE POUVAIT LES SÉPARER.
KATE WINSLET
LEONARDO DICAPRIO
7 JANVIER
TITANIC

More Facts

- Real footage of the **RMS** *Titanic* wreckage is used in the movie.
- Céline Dion's "My Heart Will Go On" is the theme music for the film. Dion won many awards for it.
- The movie made more than $2 billion dollars in theaters!

Glossary

director - a person who guides the actors and directs the performance of the script for a play or movie.

inspired - filled someone with the urge or ability to do something creative.

props - objects on a set or used by the actors performing in a play or movie.

replica - a duplication or copy, often smaller than the original.

RMS - short for Royal Mail Ship.

socialite - a person well-known in fashionable society.

Index

Online Resources

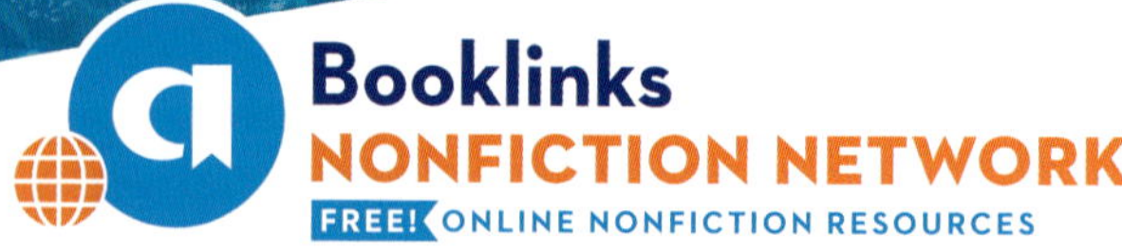

To learn more about making *Titanic* the movie, please visit **abdobooklinks.com** or scan this QR code. These links are routinely monitored and updated to provide the most current information available.